NATIVE
AMERICAN
NATIONS

# Cheyenne

**F.A. BIRD**

**CONTENT CONSULTANT: CHRISTINA GISH HILL, PHD**

Checkerboard
Library

An Imprint of Abdo Publishing
abdobooks.com

# ABDOBOOKS.COM

Published by Abdo Publishing, a division of ABDO, PO Box 398166, Minneapolis, Minnesota 55439.
Copyright © 2022 by Abdo Consulting Group, Inc. International copyrights reserved in all countries.
No part of this book may be reproduced in any form without written permission from the publisher.
Checkerboard Library™ is a trademark and logo of Abdo Publishing.

Printed in the United States of America, North Mankato, Minnesota
102021
012022

 THIS BOOK CONTAINS RECYCLED MATERIALS

Design and Production: Mighty Media, Inc.
Editor: Liz Salzmann
Cover Photograph: MATT HINSHAW/AP Images
Interior Photographs: Ad_hominem/Shutterstock Images, p. 7; Bob Sinclair/Flickr, p. 15; chapin31/
    iStockphoto, p. 25; Laurens Hoddenbagh/Shutterstock Images, p. 11; Library of Congress, pp. 17, 21;
    Paul Morse/Wikimedia Commons, p. 29; robertcicchetti/iStockphoto, p. 9; Rosanne Tackaberry/
    Alamy Photo, p. 13; Visions Service Adventures/Flickr, pp. 19, 23; William Henry Jackson/Wikimedia
    Commons, p. 27; Zack Frank/Shutterstock Images, p. 5

Library of Congress Control Number: 2021943203

**Publisher's Cataloging-in-Publication Data**
Names: Bird, F.A., author.
Title: Cheyenne / by F.A. Bird
Description: Minneapolis, Minnesota : Abdo Publishing, 2022 | Series: Native American nations | Includes
    online resources and index.
Identifiers: ISBN 9781532197178 (lib. bdg.) | ISBN 9781098219307 (ebook)
Subjects: LCSH: Cheyenne Indians--Juvenile literature. | Indians of North America--Juvenile literature. |
    Indigenous peoples--Social life and customs--Juvenile literature. | Cultural anthropology--Juvenile
    literature.
Classification: DDC 973.0497--dc23

# Contents

# CHAPTER 1

# Homelands

**The Cheyenne are made up of two groups.** These are the *Tsistsistas* (jis-jis-tus) and the *Sutaio* (suh-TYE-oh). They got the name Cheyenne from their Lakota friends. The Cheyenne originally lived north of the Missouri River in present-day Minnesota. They were fishermen and farmers. Their language is part of the **Algonquian** language family.

In the early 1600s, the Cheyenne moved west along the Missouri River to the Black Hills. They first got horses from the Kiowa around 1770. The horses allowed them to hunt buffalo on the Great Plains.

Soon after, the Cheyenne separated into northern and southern groups. The Northern Cheyenne went to present-day Montana, Wyoming, and North and South Dakota. The Southern Cheyenne went into present-day Oklahoma, Colorado, Nebraska, and Kansas.

The site of a former Cheyenne
village in western Oklahoma

# CHAPTER 2
# Society

**H**istorically, the Cheyenne lived in small **bands** of related **families.** Several times a year, the Northern and Southern bands gathered for religious and seasonal festivals.

During these special gatherings, tepees were arranged in a circle. The east end of the circle was left open to greet the morning sun. Sometimes, there were one thousand tepees in the circle. Cheyenne people still gather for festivals today and arrange their camps the same way.

The Cheyenne also had six military societies that still exist today. Any man of any age could join a military society. These societies were the Elk Soldiers, Fox Soldiers, Dog Soldiers, Shields Soldiers, Bowstrings, and Northern Crazy Dogs.

# THE CHEYENNE HOMELANDS

WASHINGTON

OREGON

IDAHO

MONTANA
Northern
Cheyenne
Reservation

WYOMING

NORTH DAKOTA

SOUTH DAKOTA

Great Plains

MINNESOTA

NEVADA

UTAH

Great Plains

NEBRASKA

COLORADO

KANSAS

Great Plains

WISCONSIN

MICHIGAN

IOWA

ILLINOIS

MISSOURI

INDIANA

OHIO

KENTUCKY

NEW
YORK

PENNSYLVANIA

WEST
VIRGINIA

VIRGINIA

MAINE

VERMONT
NEW HAMPSHIRE
MASSACHUSETTS
RHODE ISLAND
CONNECTICUT
NEW JERSEY

DELAWARE
MARYLAND
WASHINGTON, DC

CALIFORNIA

ARIZONA

NEW MEXICO

OKLAHOMA
Cheyenne-
Arapaho
Reservation

ARKANSAS

TENNESSEE

NORTH
CAROLINA

SOUTH
CAROLINA

TEXAS

MISSISSIPPI

LOUISIANA

ALABAMA

GEORGIA

FLORIDA

ALASKA

HAWAII

N
W   E
S

THE
CHEYENNE
HOMELANDS

## CHAPTER 3

# Homes

The Cheyenne lived in earthen domed houses before they moved to the Great Plains. Then, they began to live in tepees. The tepee was a good house for the **nomadic** Cheyenne. The tepees were easy to move and set up.

The Cheyenne used **travois** to move tepees and other heavy loads. The travois were pulled by horses. When the Cheyenne reached a new campsite, the women quickly set up the tepees. Tepees belonged to the women, since they were the ones who made them.

The tepee's frame was made of poles arranged in a cone shape. They were tied together at the top. The poles were then tied to stakes with rope. Then the tepee was covered with hides. A fire would be built in the center of the tepee. A flap at the top could be opened to let smoke out.

A tepee cover was made of buffalo hides sewn together. Today, tepee covers are often made of canvas.

# CHAPTER 4

# Food

**W**hen they lived in present-day Minnesota, the **Cheyenne planted corn, squash, pumpkins, beans, and tobacco.** They gathered wild rice. They also hunted duck, other marsh animals, and forest game.

When they moved to the Great Plains, the Cheyenne depended on buffalo. Buffalo were a main source of food. They also provided hides for clothing and tepees, bones for tools, and more. The Cheyenne had a use for nearly every part of the buffalo.

Cheyenne women also picked fruits and dug plant roots for stews and grilling. And the Cheyenne traded with other Native American tribes and Europeans. They traded buffalo hides for corn, tobacco, coffee, and guns.

Today, the Cheyenne manage their own buffalo herds. Buffalo meat remains an important food.

Due to overhunting by European settlers, there were only 300 wild buffalo left by the end of the 1800s. Thanks to conservation work, there are more than 200,000 buffalo roaming the plains today.

## CHAPTER 5

# Clothing

During cold months, Cheyenne men wore shirts and leggings made from **tanned** deer or elk hide. In warm weather, the men often wore **breechcloths**.

Cheyenne women wore dresses throughout the year. The dresses were made from deer or elk hide and were often decorated with **fringe**. In cooler weather, women wore leggings with the dresses. Everyone wore robes of tanned deer, elk, or buffalo hides.

Men also wore armbands and headbands and hung pouches from their waists. Women wore leather belts around their waists. A leather bag was often hung from the belt. It held important tools such as sewing needles.

Men and women also wore earrings made of bone or feather. The men wore necklaces made from talons or bear claws. Men and women wore necklaces decorated with **quills**.

A Cheyenne man wearing traditional clothing

# CHAPTER 6

# Crafts

Cheyenne women made clothes from buffalo, deer, and elk hides. The Cheyenne often used porcupine **quills** to decorate crafts and clothing. This art was called quilling. Quills were dyed using plants.

The Cheyenne had a Women's Quilling Society. Its members made tepees, dresses, leggings, pouches, and shirts. Each member was responsible for quilling a certain item. Quilling took much time and patience. The women used this time to share stories. This helped pass on tribal history and knowledge.

In the 1800s, traders brought glass beads to the Cheyenne. The beads made decorating faster and easier. But special items were still decorated with quills.

A Southern Cheyenne girl's beaded dress from the 1800s

## CHAPTER 7

# Family

Each member of a Cheyenne family had daily tasks. Women were responsible for cooking, caring for children, and taking care of the family's home. This included building the tepee.

Men were in charge of finding food and protecting their families. Children were expected to help with chores. But there was always time for play and talk among friends.

When a Cheyenne couple married, they moved into their own tepee. It was placed near the bride's mother's tepee. The husband gave meat to his mother-in-law. She gave some to all of her daughters' families who also lived nearby. The daughters' children lived together near the grandmother's tepee.

The Cheyenne used shawls to hold small children on their backs.

# CHAPTER 8

# Children

Cheyenne girls played with dolls and **cradleboards**. This got them ready to be mothers. Girls learned their tasks and crafts from their mothers, grandmothers, and aunts.

The boys played hunting and **raiding** games. This prepared them for capturing horses, hunting, and **counting coup**. Boys could join war parties when they were fourteen or fifteen years old. But they were not expected to fight. Instead, they helped the warriors before and after battle.

After dark, people gathered around the fires and sang songs. Sometimes the **elders** would tell stories that taught and entertained the children. Today, some Cheyenne children learn their language so they can tell the stories too.

A young dancer at a Northern Cheyenne celebration

# CHAPTER 9

# Traditions

One traditional Cheyenne story is about the Creator and Erect Horns. One day, all the buffalo herds disappeared from the Great Plains. The Cheyenne began to starve. The tribal leaders chose Erect Horns and his wife to go on a **vision quest** and bring the buffalo back.

Erect Horns and his wife traveled for many days. Finally, they found a hollow, magic mountain. They entered the magic mountain during a lightning storm. There, the Creator gave them the traditional teachings and the Sacred Buffalo Hat.

Erect Horns and his wife returned to the Cheyenne camp. They showed the people the Sacred Buffalo Hat. Erect Horns said the Creator told them to follow the traditional teachings and the buffalo would return.

Erect Horns showed the people how to build a Medicine Dance Lodge. This lodge was used for special ceremonies.

# CHAPTER 10

# War

**The Cheyenne fought other tribes to protect their territory.** After the Europeans brought horses to America, Cheyenne war parties also **raided** enemy villages for food, horses, and supplies. Before going to battle, the war party asked a **medicine man** to give them advice. The medicine man asked the spirits to make the war a success.

After a successful battle, the war party returned to the camp, shouting and displaying all the things they had captured. Everyone ran out to see the victory parade.

Not all battles with other Great Plains tribes involved killing. Cheyenne warriors also **counted coup**. This meant touching the enemy without killing him and then returning safely to the camp.

Before going into battle, men dyed their hair and painted their faces. Today, powwow dancers honor this tradition.

# CHAPTER II

# Contact with Europeans

In 1680, French explorer Sieur de La Salle wrote about meeting a party of Cheyenne in present-day Illinois. This was the first recorded contact between the Cheyenne and Europeans.

Later, the US government used treaties to make Cheyenne lands part of the United States. In 1861, Southern Cheyenne chief Black Kettle convinced the US government to give the Cheyenne farmland. Black Kettle hoped the new land would bring peace to his people.

But in 1864, Colonel John M. Chivington led his troops on a surprise attack against Black Kettle's camp at Sand Creek, Colorado. Many Cheyenne, including women and children, were killed during the attack. It became known as the Sand Creek Massacre.

Descendants of Sand Creek victims worked with the National Park Service to have a monument placed at the massacre site.

# CHAPTER 12

# Little Wolf & Dull Knife

**Little Wolf and Dull Knife were leaders of the Northern Cheyenne.** The US government had forced the Northern Cheyenne to live at the Southern Cheyenne Agency in present-day Oklahoma. Life at the agency was difficult. Many Cheyenne were sick and starving. In 1878, Dull Knife and Little Wolf led an escape from the agency.

The US military chased the group to present-day Nebraska. There, the group decided to separate. Little Wolf led some families north. They successfully returned to their homelands.

Dull Knife led the others to Fort Robinson in Nebraska. There, US soldiers held him and his people captive until they agreed to return to the agency.

The Cheyenne honored both Little Wolf (*left*) and Dull Knife (*right*) as heroes.

# CHAPTER 13

# The Cheyenne Today

Today, the Cheyenne are working hard to preserve their traditional teachings. They call this the "Cheyenne Way." In 1990, the US Congress passed the Native American Graves Protection and Repatriation Act (NAGPRA). The act returns sacred items to Native Americans. The act also returns burial items and remains that need to be reburied.

Senator Ben Nighthorse Campbell is Northern Cheyenne. He served in the **US Senate** from 1993 to 2005. Senator Campbell fought for laws that help Native Americans. He also helped create the National Museum of the American Indian within the Smithsonian Institution.

Today, the Southern Cheyenne are based in Concho, Oklahoma. More than 11,000 people live on 80,500 acres (32,577 ha) there. The Northern Cheyenne **reservation** is on the Tongue River in Montana. More than 6,000 people live on its 445,000 acres (180,085 ha).

US president George W. Bush greets Campbell in 2004.

# Glossary

**Algonquian**—a family of Native American languages spoken from Labrador, Canada, to the Carolinas and westward into the Great Plains.

**band**—a number of persons acting together; a subgroup of a tribe.

**breechcloth**—a piece of cloth, usually worn by men. It wraps between the legs and around the waist.

**counting coup** (KOUNT-ing KOO)—a military action where Cheyenne warriors touched the enemy without killing him, then returned safely to camp.

**cradleboard**—a decorated flat board with a wooden band at the top that protects the baby's head.

**elder**—a person having authority because of age or experience.

**fringe**—a border or trim made of threads or cords, either loose or tied together in small bunches.

**medicine man**—a spiritual leader of a tribe or nation.

**nomadic**—moving season by season to different locations to find food, water, and grazing land.

**quill**—a large, stiff feather or a sharp spine.

**raid**—to conduct a surprise attack.

**reservation**—a piece of land set aside by the government for Native Americans to live on.

**tanned**—having been made into leather by being soaked in a special liquid.

**travois** (truh-VOI)—a frame of two wooden poles tied together over the back of an animal and allowed to drag on the ground. It was used to transport loads.

**US Senate**—the upper and smaller part of the US Congress.

**vision quest**—a spiritual journey to witness the mystical or supernatural.

# ONLINE RESOURCES

**Booklinks**
NONFICTION NETWORK
FREE! ONLINE NONFICTION RESOURCES

To learn more about the Cheyenne, please visit **abdobooklinks.com** or scan this QR code. These links are routinely monitored and updated to provide the most current information available.

# Index